Self-Discovery
Practical Self-Care Strategies for Succeeding in Dating, Relationships, & Love

Rarchelle Massey-Smith

Contents

I dedicate this book to my father, whom I call Daddy; The first man to ever love me. I have always been thankful for his physical presence, but even more appreciative of what he instilled in me. He taught and showed me how to trust and depend on Jesus with everything in me; this is how I obtained my mustard seed faith. He also taught me to see from multiple perspectives and never be judgmental. But, most importantly when I was a baby, long before I could even recollect, he read as many books as he could to me in hopes that I would gain as much knowledge as possible, and that is why today, I have a thirst for knowledge and books. Your love, presence, wisdom, and hard work paid off. I am who I am because of YOU!

Thank You, Daddy!

Acknowledgments

I want to acknowledge anyone I have ever
dated or allowed to have a piece of my heart.
It is because of you that I have a story to
tell. Because of you, I learned that love is
not one size fits all but more of a series
of events that two people share and create
beautiful memories, whether the relationship
lasts a lifetime or a moment. The memories
we shared will live forever. The love we once
shared has influenced my growth and how I
give or receive love. So once again, Thank You,
and I wish you the best in all your endeavors!

Introduction

♥

I n today's society, we view love, marriages, and exclusive relationships as a waste of time, impossible, or not worth it. Staying single has become more favorable than taking a chance on a long-term relationship. When you think about taking that leap, you tune in to social media and bam, another domestic violence case or death resulting from a domestic violence case. When violence is not involved, money or battles over material things are. This results in astronomical numbers being court-ordered and paid to their ex after a breakup. The numbers are so high that even the strongest person can be left crying. Let's not forget those who are left bittered and angry due to a relationship they experienced in the past that left them scarred so profoundly that they take it out on the world.

Although all those things are devastating and hard to overcome, we must remember what love truly is. Yes, it has its share of ups and downs, but what doesn't? Love is not all of the things mentioned above, those things have transpired in the name of love, but it's unfair to call it love. The beauty of love is represented first and foremost from within. Therefore, self-discovery is essential to learning to love yourself before embarking on a lifetime of love with someone else.

Consider how much impact your relationship or previous relationships had on your happiness. For example, were you genuinely loving yourself or expecting your partner to love you first?

I have always put a lot of weight on having a relationship. I had watched my mom, who was submissive and domestic, and thought, that's what life is about; grow up, turn 18, have kids, get married, and live happily ever after. I assumed you get happiness from your spouse or boyfriend, and that's it! I never realized there is so much more love and joy to being loved when you find and partner with a suitable mate.

It never occurred to me that I was my own person with my own dreams and desires to be loved how *I* wanted to be loved. When I started having problems with my spouse, I finally realized that I was not in tune with myself even to know how I wanted to be treated. I was looking to him to compliment me and make me feel good, but I should have been giving myself those things.

I was insecure in who I was and searching for love in all the wrong places and from the wrong people, jumping in and out of relationships hoping to get happiness. Then when I became single again, I realized that when you are genuinely secure within yourself and know you are sufficient, you don't rely on others to make you feel whole.

All is fair in love and war; ultimately, anything can happen. However, choosing the wrong person to become exclusive with can be detrimental to your sense of self and, unfortunately, in some cases, dangerous to your life.

My wish is that through my experiences and tips, I can help you choose a mate wisely by getting to know yourself before getting into a relationship. Suppose you are questioning why you have not yet found the love of your life or why you always seem to choose the "wrong" one. In that case, I challenge you to keep reading and dive into understanding yourself and your expectations and identifying the red flags meant to signal that danger, or at least uncertainty, lies ahead.

My husband struggled with issues with alcohol when we met, and I saw myself going down that road as well. Although this should have been a red flag for me, a warning that we were not compatible as life partners, I ignored this and many others and pushed ahead with marrying him. Unfortunately, I had not taken the time to understand those things that were important to me or about me to know how to communicate with him or any other person I wanted to engage in a relationship with. I learned these lessons the hard way and want to share with you how you can avoid the pitfalls and tragedies of choosing the wrong mate and lay the foundation of *Self-Discovery: Practical Self-Care Strategies for Succeeding in Dating, Relationships, & Love.*

For those looking for the best ways to choose love or, better yet, to identify what you even want in a relationship, let's begin with looking at yourself.

Who Are You?

♥

Who are you? Have you ever sat down alone and asked yourself that simple question? Sometimes we get by, never really knowing who we are. When you don't learn who you are, it opens the door for you to be molded by other people's opinions and beliefs of who they think you should be. Someone's negative opinion of you can become your reality without recognizing what's happening. Often within relationships and primarily marriages, our significant others' negative opinion of us becomes our reality, which usually manifests before getting into any relationship, especially before saying, "I Do."

I suggest you take the time to get to know yourself. Discover what makes you tick. What are your pet peeves? We spend so much time getting to know other people that we never take the time to get to know ourselves. After being in a relationship for 15 years and married for ten years, I realized that I never got to know myself. I spent more than half of my life in relationships where the focus was on the person I was dating.

My self-neglect, which I like to call it, started many years ago in high school when I thought I was in love with my first serious boyfriend. Little did I know I was beginning to self-destruct. This was the best time to start discovering and forming my identity, and establishing platonic relationships would have been more beneficial at this stage of life.

Unfortunately, like many teenagers, my focus was on having a boyfriend, and not only did

I want a boyfriend, but I wanted him to be head over heels in love with me. That was it; no more exploring, no more getting to know if there were any other guys I would be interested in. In my crazy teenage mind, I thought you dated a boy with no intercourse because we were too young. Still, we would be in a relationship and wait on sex until we got married. Unfortunately, the result in most relationships, regardless of age, is sex and everything that comes with that. The pressure is high to start having sex at this time. It's also a result of dating, but let's be honest, how can a guy or woman pay for dates at this age? Save dating for your twenties, and get to know people's personalities now. That way, once you start dating, you have somewhat of an idea of what you're looking for in a mate.

Dating and even marrying the wrong person can be detrimental to a person. It could affect the rest of your life in so many ways. But wait! Before dating exclusively, take the time for self-discovery and discover what makes you tick and what you want to bring to a relationship instead of thinking about what your partner can give. Know what you are willing to deal with or not (your deal breakers).

If being alone saddened, depresses, worries, or even frightens you, you are not ready to be in any relationship. Of course! Anyone who desires to be in a relationship will feel uneasy about this. Still, it shouldn't make you feel so fearful and anxious that you make careless decisions to avoid being alone. If you don't want to spend time with yourself, why should anyone else want to spend time with you? I found myself at some point at the end of my relationships feeling like I was the victim. I didn't deserve whatever happened within the relationship to cause us to break up. As I got older and wiser, I learned that I wasn't emotionally and mentally ready for a relationship then and wasn't holding up to my part in the relationship. I was not mature enough to understand how I needed to know myself before committing to someone else. I was giving away my heart and body for what I thought was love simply because I was insecure about who I was.

Although I had two or three serious relationships before that I thought had hurt me, the big heartbreak was when my husband and I separated; I had given my 100% all to being a great wife throughout our marriage, even though our marriage eventually ended in divorce. I stand firm on my conviction and commitment to him at the time. However, I find myself bitter at times now, not because we divorced, but because my ex was too blind to at least acknowledge that he wasn't and may never be ready for a woman of my status, a woman who has the desire to be faithful to only one person, submissive, yet still independent, encouraging, uplifting, forgiving, understanding, gentle yet firm, mutable, and highly sexed. The point is that although I was all those things and believed I gave my 100%, that didn't mean my 100% was what the other person wanted or needed.

For example, some men prefer a woman who physically gets out of the house and works full-time jobs, regardless if they have a steady cash flow or not. Some like their woman home to take care of the home, children, cleaning, appointments, accounting, hobbies, and everything to help ease up some of their responsibilities after he comes home from a long, hard workday. Some may prefer to split everything down the middle; the bills, care of children, cleaning, cooking, and everything that needs to be done are divided equally. Some may prefer their partner to have a deep relationship with a higher being; some like to keep that separate from their relationship. There are many scenarios I could create, but the point here is that truly knowing who you are, what your genuine desire is in a partner, and what great qualities you already have are essential factors and needs to be understood before ever engaging in an exclusive relationship. And when I say exclusive, I am not necessarily talking about marriage but rather a relationship where your heart is exposed to the damage the wrong partner can do, which is often irreparable and traumatic.

I didn't know who I was for a long time because I was never alone long enough to understand or get to know myself fully. I was raised in a family of eight, which constantly

grew because some new niece or nephew
was born every year since I was twelve. After
15, I did my best to get to know my first
puppy/true love. Not to mention my friends
who influenced me as well. Now that I had
time to sit alone for days, months, or years,
I shifted my focus to understanding myself. I
had always been so afraid of being alone, so
I quickly jumped into the next relationship,
even at times going back to an ex. I never
allowed myself the opportunity to feel empty
and therefore discover those things about me
that make me unique.

In this season of "dating myself," as I continue
to discover the real me, I am not willing to
change the fiber of who I am; a woman who is
very merciful, compassionate, understanding,
diverse, ready to see situations from many
perspectives, and not afraid to give my all
in love, weird, who loves and trusts Jesus

with everything inside of me, eclectic, goofy, serious, loving, empathetic, emotional, loves music including gospel, rap, especially Tupac, jazz, r&b, and some country. I'm also a woman who analyzes everything and stays in my mind more than most; a dreamer, inspiring, encouraging, and serving. Although some people might not like being a server, I realize I enjoy helping and prefer a man who wants his woman to cater to him. I also know that each person is only compatible with someone who values their qualities. These characteristics influence relationships, yet we often ignore the red flags indicating a lack of compatibility. Instead, we choose the appearance, sex, or simply because they were interested in us as our barometer of "love."

Now that I am forty years old and discovering who I am, I have to stop and think about how the many relationships I have

experienced have impacted who I am.
Exclusive relationships can have a lasting
effect on who you are, whether good or bad.
In some relationships, I felt that my body
and sex were the most crucial components to
maintaining the relationship. Unfortunately,
I took that belief on to other relationships,
making sex a significant factor within the
relationship. Yes, sex is a form of intimacy, but
intimacy is more than sex. Immediate physical
gratification did not define our relationship's
level or growth.

Although I have always been focused on giving
all my love to the other person, I'm just
now fully realizing that I must love myself. I
genuinely thought that was the only way it
was supposed to be; honestly, I'm still trying
to accept that this may not be the way to be
in a happy, fulfilling relationship. Oh! I wish
it were because putting someone else's needs

before mine is so easy; seeing the good in them
no matter what is easy for me. Believing in
them and all they can do is easy. Supporting
them by any means necessary is also easy.
Being understanding and forgiving, I got it.
Cooking for them anytime they like, surprising
them with things to show I'm listening, or just
putting a smile on their face. Doing whatever
I can to make their day better, every day.
I always pray for them more than myself,
wanting them to be their best version. Now
that I am working on believing in myself, I find
that to be the hard part. Although it feels good
to shower myself with those same things, it
can be challenging.

To be in a relationship where you are fulfilled
and satisfied, you must first understand
who you are at your core. This will
require putting in the time and effort,
including meditation, alone time, openness,

and realness, to determine the depth of your soul. Unfortunately, many have hidden from their weakness, troubled past, and pain, preferring to avoid the uncomfortable emotions that come with it. For some, it feels better to ignore than deal with these things that cause discomfort and anxiety. But trust me, dealing with your issues face-on is much better than pushing them away as they eventually manifest in some form of negative outcome or response, usually during the most inopportune time.

Heal from the Past

♥

T hroughout this chapter, we will delve into ourselves to gain insight into what could trigger our negativity or insecurity within a relationship and how to overcome it to become the best version of ourselves.

These types of insecurities cause people not to know their worth and accept things that are red flags early in a relationship. In some cases, these insecurities ruin good relationships.

We learn to love through our upbringing; many parents admit they did their best but were learning as they went. Unfortunately, while most parents strive to do their best when raising their children, there are still things they do or don't do that significantly impact their children, causing negative feelings, beliefs, or emotions. However, even for those who do their best, things still slip through the cracks without them being aware of their influence on us. Some are as bad as physical abuse, incest, molestation, hunger, or as simple as being ignored and neglected. But, regardless of how minor or severe, address any concerns that may have a negative impact on you. It reminds me of split ends on hair; sometimes, it's not that bad, but left untreated, it will get worse, and depending on the severity of the split end, they may need some trimming. The damage can be remedied with special care in addressing the situation. The same applies to things that have caused us pain or to become insecure.

Addressing these issues could consist of seeking the help of a pastor, therapist, or counselor if you can't handle the problem alone. Because unresolved trauma can have a devastating and lasting effect on us, primarily if mishandled.

As for me, I was co-dependent in relationships. I was afraid to be alone. If one relationship ended, I would get into another to seek immediate gratification to not deal with the pain of a broken heart. My fear of being alone kept me in unhealthy or toxic relationships for many years. While going through a breakup, it is vital to heal and reflect on things that went right and wrong to ensure that you grow from those lessons and don't allow the same mistakes to happen in future relationships. Not taking the time to reflect and grow caused me to deflect. Even more, I started depending on men to heal my broken heart and make me feel worthy since the last relationship left me feeling unworthy. In these instances, the lesson was for me to take the time to learn after all the breakups that I was insecure and didn't think I was beautiful. I had no idea what was special about me, and I depended on a man to tell me and show me those things. I didn't know what made me unique or worthy of a man holding on to me. I should have known this before deciding to be in a relationship. If you don't see what you bring to the table, it can open up the door for you to put up with things that shouldn't be allowed, such as cheating, physical and mental abuse, and or neglect. I realized that my insecurity stemmed from childhood.

I was raised in a family of eight and was second to the youngest of six kids. The thing about growing up in large families is that your older siblings tend to push their beliefs and opinions onto the younger ones. At least, this was the case for me. From a very young age, I depended on my older siblings' views on what I should wear or how I should act, pushing away my own identity. My sisters were pretty, and I was darker than all three of them, which led to me thinking that my skin was too dark to be as appealing as theirs. Boy, was I wrong! It took me all this time to realize or see the beauty within me. It took for me to be alone and to take the time to acknowledge that I felt this way and begin to diagnose why. I had to love myself before expecting anyone else to love me.

I was insecure about being alone, so I stayed in relationships despite the red flags. I craved to be in a healthy exclusive relationship more than anything. Since I desire it so much, I often go with the flow of the person I am dating to keep him around so I won't be alone, even if

clear signs indicate that I should steer away.
I felt lost, unworthy, bored, and lonely when
I wasn't in a committed relationship. I would
even start rationalizing that I should go back
to an ex or a relationship that wasn't the best
for me, just not to be alone. I would start
thinking about how afraid I would be to cut off
someone if it meant I would have no one to
rely upon.

I eventually realized I wasn't healthy enough
mentally and spiritually to enter a relationship
with anyone except myself. My insecurities
were embedded in me so profoundly that it
would take quite some time for me to address
these issues correctly. For instance, I'm
typically nervous and timid at the beginning of
a relationship. I don't want to upset whoever
I'm dating, and I tend to go with the flow
even when red flags appear, signaling an issue
I know will rear its head later. Being secure

would make it so I won't go with the flow but trust myself enough to know when to walk away because the flow is not aligning with my spirit or goals for a relationship. So, I began the process of healing from the past.

As I became more confident, I realized that things that were a definite deal-breaker for me would now be addressed immediately. What may be a deal breaker for me may be acceptable for someone else. It's important to understand what works for you. For instance, my husband had a drinking problem, but when we met, I had just given my life to the Lord and stopped drinking. It should have been a red flag that we would not have been a good match. Now, someone who does not have a relationship with the Lord is not a good fit for me; this is a deal breaker.

Note: The more in-depth you get to know yourself, remember that you cannot change someone else. So, if you are with someone you think can change, you are setting yourself up for disappointment and sorrow.

Whatever insecurity you have that is still hindering you from happiness, It's not the other person's responsibility to fix that insecurity for you; it's up to you to dig deep and discover why you are insecure and fix it. I suggest you deal with these insecurities before presenting yourself as eligible to date. If you met someone at this stage who was ready for a mature and healthy relationship, you wouldn't represent the best version of yourself because you have deep insecurities that don't have anything to do with the relationship that needs to be resolved. No matter how much you try to push them away, they will eventually resurface until you nip those insecurities/issues in the bud.

What are you insecure about? Can you think about what you experienced, whether between your parents, siblings, relatives, or friendships, that may have caused you strife? If you can't think of anything damaging, that's great. Let's avoid creating things that aren't a problem, or are you too afraid to admit to these insecurities? Many people have some insecurity, which could stem from childhood. These insecurities could be mental, physical, emotional, or all three. We frequently push these insecurities to the back of our minds to protect ourselves from the pain, but eventually, they resurface.

Have you ever talked to someone who mentioned some of the things they witnessed as a kid which affected their ability to be in a relationship? You may have thought this was an excuse, but many people with childhood trust issues fear being in a relationship. Some people don't have to dig deep to find their insecurities because they have used them as an excuse or a crutch their entire lives. In that case, finding a way to overcome them and move forward with life is critical. The first step is to be true to what makes you insecure or afraid and address the issue head-on.

So once again, I ask you, what are your insecurities or pain that keep you from living a peaceful and joyous life? What topic usually upsets or makes you uneasy during discussions or arguments with friends, relatives, or lovers? Is there anything deeper than what's showing up on the surface that may need some delving into? Some of our insecurities are embedded so deep that it will take some serious digging to discover how some problems may have impacted our lives, causing us to deflect or, better yet, just not be the best we can be as individuals or within a relationship. So take your time and think about it.

Are You Self-Reliant and Fulfilled?

♥

Can you take care of yourself? Can you make it if all your resources disappeared today? Sometimes we get into relationships before we become independent, which usually leads to codependency. We choose to get married because we love our partners and can't see ourselves living without them. It should never be because we need them to take care of us. Sure, back in the day, women would get pregnant very young, drop out of school, get married, and depend on their husbands to care for them. Even though these men were great at managing their homes, I often saw generation after generation taking their wives for granted. After all, they knew they depended on them and couldn't stand on their own two feet because they usually continued to get pregnant. Although their marriages typically lasted a lifetime, the women endured so much disrespect because they knew it would be tough to leave their husbands and survive without education. Although women found themselves stuck with their husbands, men felt stuck as well because they didn't want their wives to take their children away from them and didn't want to pay child support.

Times have changed, and there are typically not only one but two breadwinners. Regardless if you decide to become a stay-at-home parent or a domestic partner, it is still imperative to become independent and know how to take care of yourself whether you have to or not. Being independent helps build your self-worth and gives you the security to move freely. I have listened to and seen many people stay in horrible situations only because they didn't think they could survive without the help of their partner or significant other. I also have friends and relatives who chose a partner, not because of compatibility or love but because they wanted someone to depend on to care for them. After all, they were co-dependent. Within a healthy, committed relationship, individuals depend on each other for things, but no one should be forced to care for their partner because they lack independence. Eventually, this can burden the independent one, or the co-dependent individual could feel powerless.

Nevertheless, becoming financially independent is crucial for having a healthy relationship. Of course, there will be times when everyone needs some form of help, but the ultimate goal is to take care of yourself financially without the assistance of anyone else. Taking care of yourself financially during the various stages of your life will consist of different things. For example, if you still live at home with your parents, you may not have to pay rent but may have enough finances to take care of yourself in other ways, such as food, clothing, car, car insurance, and wants. There is nothing wrong with this, especially if you are just casually dating. Still, your goal is to supply all your needs with shelter included before taking on a big step, such as moving in or marrying someone. Some people prefer to have a roommate instead of living alone, and this is ok, but ask yourself, "If my roommate suddenly moved out, could I instantly afford to pay all the bills, or would I have to make accommodations?" If you can instantly afford it, you are independent because you can care for yourself. Still, if the answer is no, you are technically not independent, which is the goal before ever moving in or marrying your companion.

It is ok to date while in pursuit of becoming independent; remember to take it slow and keep your focus on independence. Continue to focus on becoming financially independent before becoming economically responsible for kids or anyone else. Once we become official, we often lose focus and begin to turn our focus on goals as a couple, which is ok as long as your individual goals don't take the back burner. I know numerous people, especially females, that will put 100 percent into helping their partner reach their goals, cheer them on, and believe in them, but when I ask what it is in their life that they are passionate about, they become speechless. They don't have many goals outside being a parent or a better half to their partner. Understandably, you may have the role of a parent and wife, and those roles are a priority. However, to be the best at those roles, you must first be the best at your number one priority, which is YOU.

Being independent builds morale. If you don't have goals to better yourself, you will also lack enthusiasm, leading to unhappiness and dissatisfaction.

Being self-fulfilled requires a lot of dedication, commitment, and hard work at making yourself a number one priority without becoming selfish to the world. You don't want to become arrogant or too greedy, but you want to give yourself the best treatment you possibly can. Let's put it like this. If you give your all in relationships and can't wait to meet Mr. Right in hopes of treating him like a king, then your job before meeting Mr. Right is to treat yourself as if you are the queen he is expecting to gain by choosing you. Don't wait until you are his woman to become the best version of you; start now. One of the best ways to become self-fulfilled is by achieving goals, big and small. Starting with small goals helps build your morale while working towards those big goals. For example, if you want to start saving but need more extra cash, begin with something feasible, such as saving $15 per month for six and twelve months. That doesn't seem like much, but self-control, commitment, and dedication make you feel good once that goal is reached, and you start thinking about what you could do if you put your mind to it and stay consistent. This applies to any plan you may have, whether physical, emotional, financial, spiritual, or career-related.

Whether you are happy in your current career or not, never stop your brain by keeping up with the times and learning about something through reading and classes, there is always something new to learn; this world is full of so many things to do and discover. While becoming independent, you should set short- and long-term goals.

Spoil Yourself

♥

How many times have you been in a relationship and sacrificed your wants and needs to ensure you are fulfilling the desires and needs of your significant other? When dating someone, it is essential to consider the needs and wishes of that person. But before fulfilling someone else's needs and wants, take care of yourself first. Have you heard the sayings, take care of home first, or Charity starts at home? YOU Are Home. If you are not giving yourself the self-love you deserve and need, you will expect your significant other to fulfill those wants and needs, which can lead to codependency.

Your partner should supplement, not be your supplier, in meeting all your wants and needs. For example, happiness is something that you should have or strive to maintain regardless if you are in a relationship or not.

You should not expect happiness from your partner; it should come from within. Although this sounds like common sense, I've seen many people expecting happiness from within their relationship, and in each of those relationships, they were consistently let down. I was that person. I expected my husband or whomever I was dating to provide me with happiness, and of course, I was let down each time. Many years later, I realized that I should've been spoiling myself to get everything I wanted. Spoiling yourself is not selfish and should be done before dating anybody, especially before making it exclusive. When pampering yourself with the things you like, you show the world, but most importantly, whoever you decide to date, that you are important and worth the finer things in life. If you are not willing to buy the Chanel bag, diamonds, or book the trip, why should you expect someone else to deem you worthy of spending a lot of money on you when you are not willing to do it for yourself? I'm not suggesting you spend beyond your means, but I am saying that you put yourself in a financial position to have a surplus of money and, with that extra, do something nice for yourself often. **Note:** you should only consider dating if your finances allow you to do simple things like get a haircut, get your nails or hair done, or buy a nice outfit for the month. These simple things are beneficial in making you feel good about yourself.

I knew a guy who was separated from his wife and desperately wanted her back, but she refused to go back once she caught him having sex with a woman in the bed of the home they shared. He said it didn't mean anything; he just needed sex. If you can't afford or are unwilling to pay for a hotel to protect the home you want your wife to return to, you should not be having sex. Especially when your wife still has a key. Before dating or getting your sexual desires fulfilled, make sure your finances allow you to take that special someone on a date. Your number one priority should be to afford the things you like.

Spoiling yourself is not limited to financial things; it also includes doing something you enjoy or things that relax you. For example, reading a good book, watching movies, taking a relaxing bubble bath, meditating, watching sports, making music, listening to music, or whatever you discover makes you happy. During this time of spoiling yourself, if you don't know what makes you happy, this would be the time to find out what that may be. Some people know early in their life what they enjoy doing and want they want to do for a living, and others need time alone, spoiling themselves to engage in this self-discovery. Although dating and spoiling myself felt strange and out of character for someone such as myself who has always been in a relationship, contrary to my beliefs, it has been rewarding and beneficial. But what does dating yourself mean? Dating/spoiling yourself looks like giving yourself everything you have been looking for and expecting from a partner. I went out of my way to do nice things and invest in myself, including getting nice clothes, practicing self-care, and taking myself out for a nice dinner! Focusing on *me* gave me the confidence I had always sought from another person. Once you are in a relationship, it takes away much of your focus on yourself, making it challenging to discover what makes you tick. Nothing is worse than getting married only to realize that you lost yourself in your marriage. You only lose yourself if you decide to get married before genuinely knowing who you are and what you want. Once you start spoiling yourself regularly, you will find it challenging to stop.

The very first time I started spoiling myself was shortly after a rough breakup. I was in my early twenties. It took me a while to move on and realize that the relationship was over and not worth fighting for, and once I came to that realization, I began to focus on myself. I started to get my hair and nails done every other week, and those simple things made me feel good about myself. My hair had grown longer than ever and was manageable, healthy, bouncy, and flowing in the wind. My nails were impeccable. I would get compliments all the time about my hair and my nails. The icing on the cake was when I finally decided to get braces to correct my overbite. It was a lousy overbite because I sucked my index and middle finger simultaneously until I was ten. My overbite was an insecurity that I had dealt with since grade school. I often covered my mouth with my hand whenever I laughed or talked so my teeth wouldn't show. I finally decided to face my fear of getting braces and the pain I may experience. I also decided I was worth the $4000 to correct something that made me feel so insecure: braces, no major surgery, and a payment plan; I started questioning why I had waited so long. I knew it was because I pushed myself to the back burner and made my whole focus on a relationship, and I didn't matter as much as the relationship did.

Another major thing I started spoiling myself with at that time was inner peace, which I developed by connecting with my higher being. I attended church regularly to learn more about the Word; I read my Bible, prayed, and fasted. With all the things I was doing to spoil myself, I began to feel like a new person, and it was as if I was finally truly living the way God designed for me to live. I was genuinely enjoying my life. There were moments when I would think about having a spouse and children, but overall I was content, confident, and at peace. It was something long overdue. I had been working since I was sixteen, and instead of spoiling myself, I was satisfying the guy with whom I shared a relationship. I was happy and walked around with a new outlook on life UNTIL.

I found myself back in an exclusive relationship again. After spoiling myself for nearly two years, I fell back into the trap. This time I fell even harder. I slowly stopped doing everything for myself and started doing what I always do in exclusive relationships focusing on the guy I'm dating or the relationship, goodbye to sweet ole me. If only I had enjoyed that time.

I always wonder what it is about me that would make me do anything for my mate but the bare minimum for myself. I would make up excuses for not spending so much on that diamond ring, luxury car, big ole house, massage, pamper day, hair, new clothes, or trip. I would make up excuses about how I didn't need it. It would take me a long time to convince myself I was worthy of that costly item or of pampering myself. I would only splurge when I was upset or received a lump sum. I didn't have children then and was working full-time management jobs. I wasn't saving for a goal, either, so I had enough money to do nice things for myself. Unfortunately, I didn't deem myself worthy of getting my nails and hair done. It's a shame I received my first professional pedicure when I was forty once I truly started spoiling and dating myself.

Although dating and spoiling myself felt strange and out of character for someone such as myself who has always been in a relationship, contrary to my beliefs, it has been rewarding and beneficial. But what does dating yourself mean? Dating/spoiling yourself looks like giving yourself everything you have been looking for and expecting from a partner. I went out of my way to do nice things and invest in myself, including getting nice clothes, practicing self-care, and taking myself out for a nice dinner! Focusing on *me* gave me the confidence I had always sought from another person. Once you are in a relationship, it takes away much of your focus on yourself, making it challenging to discover what makes you tick. Nothing is worse than getting married only to realize that you lost yourself in your marriage. You only lose yourself if you decide to get married before genuinely knowing who you are and what you want. Once you start spoiling yourself regularly, you will find it challenging to stop.

Sometimes within a marriage, one spouse, usually the one who ends up feeling lost, tends to put their spouse's needs above their own, which is neither healthy nor does it lead to happiness. Take care of yourself above all things because you matter. Giving everything you have to offer before giving to yourself does not lead to equilibrium, which is the goal when giving and receiving within a relationship.

Enjoy Being Single

♥

Being single is an exciting time that shouldn't be rushed. It's during this time that you become more in touch with yourself. You don't have to consider another person for making decisions during this time. Whatever you want to do, you can do it with no questions asked. During this time, you find true independence and discover what you truly love doing. It's when you find your passion and can work on becoming the best version of yourself. Unfortunately, I waited until after I said, "I do," to realize I never enjoyed the moment of being single. I was either afraid to get to know myself or didn't like myself enough to spend time alone. Whatever the case, I eventually realized that time alone was time to fine-tune myself while being in a relationship with myself to become my best version.

During the first moment you arrive in the world, there are several people in the room waiting to welcome you. You quickly adjust to a life where people are always around, there will be people anxiously waiting to be in your presence, and it's pretty constant from there on in. Not to say that having many people around is terrible. However, never spending quality time alone could hinder your ability to know yourself and understand who you are. The point is that people will always be around as long as you live, and being alone for a while can be beneficial when you see all the perks of being single and alone has to offer. Sometimes we fail to take advantage of the quality time we have when we're single, and this is truly an advantage if seen from other perspectives besides being lonely. What we do with the time we are alone is what truly matters. Remember that this time is not forever, but once you find your true soulmate, that time can be forever. Therefore, enjoy singlehood because it's only temporary.

I can still remember being single after a devastating breakup which is typically such a hard time for someone like myself to enjoy. I wanted to be a wife. That is what I thought women do once they finish high school. It was all I saw in my future. It's surprising how hard it is for me to enjoy being single. You have to slap the greatness of being single in my face, maybe even twice, for me to realize that it's a moment of happiness that should be lived and enjoyed. But, unfortunately, during this time, many women dread it or get depressed, thinking it's a sad stage because they don't have someone special in their lives, forgetting that they get to spend their time with the most special person in the world—themselves. During this time, you can express yourself without apologizing. Think about it, how many times did you spend your Friday or Saturday evenings with someone doing what they wanted to do, and you convinced yourself that you enjoyed it just because you were able to be around that one person you thought was incredible at the time? Making your own decisions is more valuable than you can imagine. Most people think it's a given, but you yearn for independence once your decision-making depends on someone else.

Yes, there were things I would've adjusted, but overall I found myself amazed at how my mom could run a house full of kids and tend to my dad's every need effortlessly. I saw her as more than a wife. It required specific skills, passion, dedication, loyalty, and an intimate relationship with a higher being. I knew I had all that, which made being single a pass time until I found someone to enjoy being in a relationship with. Unbeknownst to me then, I desired someone I enjoyed being with but failed to ensure that the person I chose could receive the type of love I wanted to offer because it was rare and beautiful. As a result, I was always in a rush to leave this stage of life every time I was single.

There were days when I did enjoy the peace that came with being single and the freedom, but it never felt as fulfilling as I felt in a committed relationship. Well, to think back, there were fewer fulfilling days than days filled with heartache and pain, but when I was single, I focused on those rare fulfilling days rather than the multitude of painful days.

Being single is an excellent time of your life; it's like when a child rushes to become an adult. Can you remember how easy it was when you were a child or teenager without all the responsibilities of being an adult? This same ideology applies to being single. When you are single, you get to choose what to do, when, and how you want to do it freely, without influences from someone else or worrying about what someone else thinks about your choices. When you think about it, we go from our parents controlling our lives and sometimes straight into a relationship where our significant others greatly influence who we are without knowing how to enjoy ourselves and make good decisions on our behalf. Although I am not singling out men vs. women, men seem to have an easier time being single than women.

Suppose I rush my time of being single and seeking or entertaining men in hopes of being in a relationship. In that case, I would be doing a disservice to myself because I'm not emotionally strong enough to date right now. I still have a couple of things to work on in the process of becoming the best version of myself and being able to influence a relationship positively.

Establish Good Friendships

♥

Congratulations! You have officially started dating yourself. Now it's time to introduce the new and improved you to your friends, make more friends, and establish platonic relationships.

You don't get to choose who your family will be. Your parents are automatically assigned to you; therefore, your grandparents, siblings, cousins, aunts, and uncles become your family tree, whether you like it or not. Since we don't have a choice in choosing our family, we can quickly feel frustrated and irritated by them for various reasons such as their personality clash with yours, they are bossy and mean, to name a few. But, regardless of what about them drives you insane, you love them anyway and learn to get along with them or love them from a distance. You still wish you could choose your own family occasionally, but you're stuck no matter what.

Although you are stuck with the family you're born into, the good news is: you don't have to be stuck with your second family, called friends. You have a choice in choosing your friends, and choosing good friends can lead to a friendship that lasts a lifetime and turns into a bond that can't be broken as if they were born into your family bloodline. Learning to select friends that are good for you is a prerequisite for later on when choosing a mate.

Establishing good friendships before becoming exclusive is vital because it allows you to learn how to interact with someone who comes from another upbringing than yours, which means they will have a different point of view than the point of view that was taught or maybe even imposed on you by your family you were born into. Being able to have different points of view while still respecting each other points of view is one of the values that come from a good friendship. It teaches that even though you believe something is this way, I understand and respect that there can be another way of seeing things.

Establishing good friendships also helps us to learn to compromise and not be selfish. You quickly learn that you and your chosen friend have similarities and many things in common, but you still have differences. It's through those differences that you learn how to compromise and take turns doing something together that you both equally enjoy. This is the foundation of establishing give and take within a relationship that plays a vital role in your future intimate relationships where emotions can interfere with being reasonable.

Building platonic relationships doesn't require sexual intimacy, which allows you to learn how to interact with people of the opposite sex without becoming romantic. It's beneficial for growth because it helps you see things from contrasting perspectives of the opposite sex. Sometimes men process things differently than women. When you are in an exclusive relationship, the intimacy can cloud your ability to listen and understand these differences thoroughly. Learning how to have conversations and friendships without being intimate is essential.

Many guys will be interested in pursuing you for various reasons, but more so now than ever because you are living the best version of yourself, which shows to everyone who meets you. You are healed, self-aware, and enjoying what life has to offer, and that makes you happy, or what I like to call living in the light, which exudes happiness, and everyone wants to be around happiness. This time can be short-lived if you move too fast and allow someone still in darkness to embark on a relationship with you. That is why only platonic relationships and friendships are essential at this stage.

Discover Your Passion!

♥

All is fair in love and war. You may have heard this idiom at some point in your life. I didn't understand it when I first heard it, but eventually, I realized that it is one truism. This idiom means no matter how good or bad you view your relationship, anything can go, rather it's fair or not. For example, can you remember when you had to break up even though you didn't want to? Or when you no longer found your partner interesting but felt terrible about breaking up when they were still interested in you?

Regardless of how much effort you put into your relationship or how much you love the other person, it can still not work out in your favor or how you prefer it to work. When a relationship ends, it tends to get the best of us, leaving you feeling hopeless with no direction or passion to live. Although you can't escape the heartache that may come with being in a relationship or a bad breakup, you can alleviate some of the pain by living in your purpose before even establishing a long-term relationship.

For many hopeless romantics, their passion is everything pertaining to their relationships, so imagine what happens if a relationship ends. Of course, when you are living truly in your passion, you still will deal with the ups and downs that can come with a relationship or a breakup, but you understand there are positive things that excite and drives you outside of your relationship. We often expect someone else to bring joy, not realizing that happiness comes from within. And

I searched for years to discover my passion, I even moved across the country in hopes that I would find a drive outside of being in a relationship, and ironically, I came back home to pursue a relationship, which resulted in two beautiful boys. However, I felt passionless outside of the relationship and being a mother. What I found odd about being a wife and a mother is, again, it's what I thought I always wanted. It had been my passion since I was a young girl, but unbeknownst to me, those were just roles I desired in my life, but not my true passion. My true passion would be something that will reach more than a few people, such as my family, but my reason for being here on earth is to influence and help many people in ways that I couldn't even imagine.

Sample questions to ask yourself when trying to discover your passion?

- What excites you?

- What does your Ideal day look like?

- If money was no object, What would you do?

- What qualities do you admire in others?

- If life stopped today, What would you regret not doing?

- What did you want to be when you were younger?

- How do you like to relax?

- What do you like doing in your spare time?

- If you could work under the tutelage of anyone worldwide for one year, who would it be and why?

- What makes you unique?

Get to Know Potential Prospects - Intro to Dating

❤️

When we start dating, especially those of us who are hopeless romantics, we fall in love quickly and want to become exclusive. Unfortunately, we do not take the time to see if there are red flags. Unless you are healed, as discussed in previous chapters, and a healthy and self-reliant individual, it is easy to fall and fall hard. When a man is not really for us, we start doing so much extra to make him fall in love too. That's not how it works; it is supposed to come naturally, not you forcing him or pushing him to stay. Getting to know potential prospects can be an enlightening experience, and it doesn't require getting intimate but becoming comfortable communicating and learning what different people have to offer.

Once you start dating, the very first prospect often stops you in your tracks. I'm not saying this person may not be the one, but explore what is out there. Choosing to become exclusive quickly takes away from the experience of learning about your partner or even if that prospect should become your exclusive partner. Just because someone is a great father, sexy, intriguing, or well-put-together doesn't mean they are the one for you. He may have some characteristics or appearances you like, but that doesn't mean he is a match for you.

He could be, but if many other red flags have presented themselves or the person genuinely doesn't want to move in the same direction as you, you may want to keep him as a potential but continue with getting to know other people. I never really took the time to get to know potential prospects when I was younger. If I was single and met someone I vibed with, I would immediately choose to become exclusive. There was no more dating or taking the time to get to know each other. It started with an attraction, and If I felt a positive way around that person, and they felt the same, then sooner rather than later, we were having intercourse and in an exclusive relationship. Not only did I fail to get to know that person to see if he was a reasonable prospect, but I also stopped exploring other prospects.

We often need to find out their attributes before dating them exclusively. We like what we see; that feeling takes over, and nothing else matters. There are times, and I know I fall victim to doing this when we don't want to be lonely or think about our ex, so we move forward with someone just to help ease the pain, which is usually called the rebound guys or I like to say your partner by default. No one should be your partner by default; take your time to yourself to heal and grow before becoming exclusive.

What is Your Communication Style?

♥

Many friends and couples have approached me as their mediator during a heated discussion, debate, or disagreement simply because I have always been a good listener. It always appeared evident from the outside looking that both individuals were saying the same thing, just in different ways or discussing something neither of them was right about. I like to call it miscommunication between teams. So I pushed for them to, most importantly, acknowledge that they see things about this subject differently and to learn from each other. Learning about differences on an issue can teach you another view, or consider leaving that topic for your platonic friendships with whom you share common ideas and points of view.

Communication is an essential feature in my relationships, right after trust. I know trust is vital for me, but I can trust you with all my being, and that's great. But every single time we interact and need to get the point across or want something, all that has to be done through communication.

There was this guy I had a big crush on, and we dated for over two years. For some reason, it appeared as if we were speaking two different languages. I know there can be a difference between how a woman communicates and how a man communicates, but this was different. Most heart-to-heart discussions led to an argument, each of us feeling we weren't being understood or completely shutting down the conversation. In those moments, I realized we had the desire to be together, but neither one of us was going to be heard throughout the relationship. Not because we didn't want to understand each other but because we couldn't understand how we communicated.

Since I did not want the relationship to end, I started looking at our zodiac signs and how it plays a role in communication. There must be a reason for our inability to communicate and some way to fix this minor thing. But honestly, communication is not insignificant in any relationship. It's the foundation of a relationship.

I learned that I'm an earth sign and he was a fire sign. As an earth sign, I prefer to communicate my feelings, and fire signs prefer to avoid the issue, hoping it will go away or fix itself. If not, then they process it within themselves. Understanding that your astrological sign has something to do with the way you process information would make it clear that you can't change the way a person is; you either can learn to communicate in ways that both signs understand and respect each other or you find someone more compatible with your communication style.

Many years ago, I worked for a company with over 400 employees. One day they had a psychologist come in and test each employee to learn their preferred form of communication. Four colors classify each communication type; blue, red, yellow, or green.

• Blue represents a person who likes to get straight to the point with no small talk involved.

• Red means the person wants to talk and be personal before receiving information.

• Yellow represents the person who loves a lot of details, paperwork, and facts when receiving information.

• Green was open to small talk and details before receiving data.

The reasoning behind the testing was to find out each person's communication style.

Once you know your communication style and how you prefer to receive information, that color sticker will hang outside each cubicle or office. Your co-workers and managers should consider your communication style whenever they interact with you. It helped everyone to communicate more smoothly.

We also learned that the old saying, "Treat others how you want to be treated," can be misleading. Instead, treat others according to how they would like to be treated. For example: if you are the type of person that needs time alone and processes issues before discussing the problem, whereas another individual wants to address the issue immediately, respect that this individual needs time before communicating instead of treating them the way they would prefer to be treated by discussing it instantly.

This concept was something I had to learn within my marriage. My husband liked to process his thoughts first, and early in our marriage, I found it frustrating not to address our issues immediately to nip them in the bud. I found that I was invading his space which could be annoying for the person who needs time to themselves. I thought he was inconsiderate, but it was just his communication style.

Regardless of your communication style, understanding the communication style of the person you want to be exclusive with is essential.

When times get tough, and believe me, they will; how will you and your partner communicate? Will you communicate effectively with respect and dignity no matter the problem? Some things can transpire that cause frustration and anger, sometimes even infidelities. I don't condone cheating and never will, but what matters more than cheating is how the person who cheated handles and cares for the person they cheated on. How they communicate about their infidelities and handle the other person's emotions and feelings matters because it shows how they will communicate during good and bad times and if they can at least say the things needed during the vulnerable part.

Are You Compatible?

♥

Diversity is great; it helps us see from other perspectives, but let's be honest, diversity can also cause many disagreements/arguments in a relationship. When two people decide to become exclusive, they bring together two different upbringings and try to collaborate as one. If these two upbringings are on opposite sides of the spectrum, seeing your partner's point of view can become challenging, leading to disagreements, arguments, and often someone's needs not being met. Unmet needs can become detrimental to a relationship. I learned that when communicating with your partner, it is essential that both individuals can see from each other's perspective.

Doing so helps to avoid misunderstandings and a failed relationship. These misunderstandings start feeling like you're arguing until you are blue in the face, but your partner can't understand where you are coming from, no matter how you try to explain. When this happens repeatedly, someone in the relationship tends to shut down and give up or stop trying to resolve or explain. That's not good. No one who wants to be in a healthy exclusive relationship prefers to misunderstand or be misunderstood by their partner intentionally.

We are all born with various ways of seeing things; this makes us diverse. Those different ways of seeing things are perspectives. The goal is to become exclusive with someone who can see your view or at least be open to understanding your perspective. I have observed couples arguing over a subject they both agreed on and wanted a positive outcome, but somehow frustration kicked in within one of them, needing to be understood. Are you sure you know the person you want to become exclusive with? Yes, you have been spending a lot of time together, and it may seem like it's time to become exclusive, but wait! Have you been around them when they're upset? What about upset with you? How about when they have mistreated you? How did they handle it? In these types of moments, a person shows their true colors, and when they do, it's best to make sure the colors that are revealed are colors you both like. In other words, how your partner treats you when upset matters a lot. These situations are a tell-all of how the overall relationship will go.

Many things will happen throughout life that will cause frustration within individuals, and when you are upset, you tend to take those frustrations out on the person closest to you. Sure, there will be times when an argument can get slightly ugly, depending on the content. Still, when it comes to being exclusive and sharing your life with someone, it is vital to have the ability to contain that ugliness because treating the person with whom you are exclusive with care should always be a number one priority. Relationships are like very fragile glass; what's left once the glass is broken or shattered? Whoever you decide to become exclusive with needs to value you like an expensive piece of glass they never want to break. It is then when they will be most careful with caring for you, regardless if times are good or bad.

Now, again these things come with maturity and self-assurance. If you or the person you become exclusive with are not mature enough and haven't done enough self-discovery and become self-reliant, then handling something so fragile is not suggested now. It would be like giving an expensive vase to a 5-year-old. They will try their best to keep up with it, but they are young, inexperienced, and immature enough to handle something delicate, fragile, and expensive. The same applies to an adult who has yet to take the time to discover within themselves how they handle situations.

You may think you're compatible because you have one or two things in common, but it's more depth than just having things in common. Everybody will find something they share with someone else if they are looking for it. Now, it's cool you have things in common; let's not just run on this. Sometimes, you may mistake good conversations or fun nights for compatibility. Just because you have a few things in common doesn't mean you are compatible. You may enjoy someone's company, and since you enjoy spending time with that someone, you believe you are compatible, but that might not be the case. We try our best to stay ignorant that the person we've been getting to know or dating for a while may not be the one we're compatible with. Yes, they have great qualities and good conversation, but that isn't enough when choosing someone to become exclusive with. They could become a lifetime friend, but compatibility is more than infatuation or having a few things in common when spending a lifetime together. It requires someone who gets you and understands your flaws and all, and still sees the beauty within you. Someone who doesn't try to change who you are but brings out the best in you.

This guy I once knew was so easy to talk to, funny, and took care of his business. He was honest, handsome, strong, reliable, fun, energetic, wise, in shape, and just pleasing to the eye. We could talk for hours about everything. Once he spoke of tarrying for the holy ghost. I thought he was the one because no one ever shared that similar experience as me. I figured he must know God on a deep level, the same as me, and that was something else I truly admired about him. I knew this had to be it, but truthfully we weren't compatible, and the more I pushed us to be, the more it became evident. The role I wanted for myself and what he thought I should be were opposites.

For example, he wanted a career-oriented woman who was money and position driven, and that wasn't me. I enjoy the role of being a domestic partner. I also like to make money and do things that put me in positions to live comfortably, but I'm not driven for positions within companies or big houses and millions of dollars. All that is great, but it doesn't move me. I'm driven by love and enjoy being a helpmate to my partner while standing by his side, back, and front as a supportive and involved partner. I'm a behind-the-scenes girl who allows her work to speak for itself. If offered the option of $500 or a day of quality time, I would choose the day of quality time any day. I'm probably more compatible with a guy who desires to come home to a clean house with a cooked meal and is ready to talk about his day and get all his needs taken care of.

Even though I'm supportive and domestic, I still like to carry my weight. I have a bachelor's degree in psychology and have worked for over ten years as a manager. I have an income, yes it could be more, but I prefer having my time over a lot of money. I am working on making more money by putting my passions to work for me. I knew once I had kids that I didn't prefer to work 40 hours away from home while trying to raise kids, so whoever I date will have to understand that I never want to work a typical 40-hour work week. I have to work for myself or have a flexible schedule. I have always paid all my monthly bills on my own, with my income; I prefer most of my time to be in my home and not outside the house. That doesn't mean if I get some creative idea, I don't want to embark on it. I like to go with the flow as long as I keep enough income to pay all bills while being creative. I also have kids, and this person didn't want any kids, which is a big deal-breaker; we probably should've stopped right there because that is a true red flag that becoming exclusive in the future wouldn't work.

I didn't want to change my mind about working a typical 40-hour workweek, and I didn't want anyone to convince me otherwise. So let me make myself clear. I don't see anything wrong with someone working a regular 9-5 or 7-3 Monday-Friday job. On the contrary, I push myself and anyone unhappy within their careers to do something they are passionate about and love doing, which may come in any form of work, depending on the individual.

Now that I'm divorced and single again, I figured the dating scene should be a lot better than when I was in my early twenties, but I found out it is even more complicated at this age than in my twenties.

One reason is that now people are more sure of who they are or what they want and don't want. Many people have decided they prefer to stay single because they find peace and solitude in being single, and they never want to experience the madness and pain that frequently come with being in an exclusive relationship. Some know they will never be married again or cohabitate, but they are open to dating and becoming intimate with one particular person. Some want to be close but leave all the labels at the door. I still believe in the union of marriage and dating exclusively with titles, even cohabitation. I admit I had my share of devastating relationships and breakups, but through the pain, I still can't let go of my desire for a meaningful exclusive connection. But I've often been told that if I want something exclusive, even with guys that don't prefer an exclusive relationship, I must step up and force the connection on the person. That is not me, and if I have to do that now that I'm in my forties, I'm in trouble because that's not what I will do.

If you need to know where your partner stands on issues such as these, you can use more time to get to know each other by having these discussions during dates and phone conversations when you're still getting to know each other. One way of digging deeper into the ideal relationship you and your partner desire is to ask questions about who they view as an ideal or the worst couple out there. People often look to celebrities' lives and the tabloids for this information. But, if he says a specific famous couple has the ideal relationship and you think they are miserable and misaligned, should he be a good match for you? Are your ideas aligned? Is his impression of a healthy relationship too different than yours? Although it may seem juvenile to talk about others this way, it is great to hear how he defines a healthy relationship and if he is right for you.

Savor The Moment

♥

T here is always something to enjoy in every stage of a relationship. Sometimes, we rush the current moment to get to the next plateau of the dating cycle. I have been guilty of this ever since I started dating. I found myself enjoying the time I was spending with one fantastic guy. We didn't have labels such as girlfriend or boyfriend, but we spent all our free time talking or being together. There was so much understanding, communication, laughter, love, freedom, and growth within our bond.

Yet still, I found myself wondering why we didn't have defined labels to explain what we were to each other. It was clear we were two adults who enjoyed the company of one another with no pressure or expectations. We allowed whatever special bond we had to flow wherever it decided to go without using rules or force. So I naturally wanted to push for more of the traditional titles or labels two people who spend a lot of time together usually assign to each other. Still, in my heart, I felt comfortable with our moving pace. Sometimes, I thought we were ready to take it to the next level. However, I found that I still needed to accomplish things within myself before moving to a committed relationship.

These types of moments are pivotal times to continue as close friends while constantly getting to unravel the depths of each other. Embrace this time, and everything you can learn and grow from these moments will never return. If the relationship lasts for a while, you will find yourself reminiscing on these days and wishing you could return in time. Take photos, create memorable moments, and experience this moment without worrying about the future. While exclusively dating someone, learning to be in an exclusive relationship without sacrificing who you are is essential. You have to learn how to balance your own time and life outside your relationship while still managing quality time within the relationship.

Can you think back on a relationship you once were in when it was so amazing at the beginning, and you felt like you still were balancing your life, and then at some point, you started giving too much of yourself to the other person that you neglected your own needs? So many people become exclusive and throw everything that doesn't pertain outside their partner to the back burner without realizing they no longer participate in any activities on their own or with their friends. Of course, you will have less time, but you should only put your all into yourself.

Let It Flow

♥

It is normal to expect a series of things to happen shortly after becoming exclusive, including vacations, marriage, houses, kids, investments, and all that good stuff. Still, that time will come on its own and doesn't need to be facilitated by anyone; instead, it should just flow. People, especially women, often have this misconceived notion that we must be married and have a big house with at least two kids by a certain age, or it will never happen. It's as if we are in a race to get into debt and lose our freedom. Having kids, a big house on the hill, and a spouse comes with a lot of commitment and responsibility. Although it can be well worth it, many people wish they would've taken their time and prepared more before making that colossal step.

Some of it can become or feel like a huge mistake when rushed or done with the wrong person. These goals can be on your to-do list; there's no specific time to do it. Each person and situation is unique. For example, I found myself pressuring a guy I had been in an exclusive relationship with for four years and dating for close to seven years that it was time to get married because I wanted kids. I felt I was getting too old and desperately wanted to start a family. At this time, I was 29 years old, and I had always wanted to have children. I wanted to have kids right out of high school but knew my father would be disappointed, so I deferred that dream and waited till I met the so-called one or made the one I was with the one and pressured him to marry me, flaws and all. Pressuring anyone to do things they are not ready for can and usually does backfire. You may temporarily get what you want, but when deciding to have children or get married, both parties should be consenting adults without any pressure, ultimatums, or other trickery.

Those big choices in life will last a lifetime. It should be done with complete submission and careful planning. Red flags should never be ignored, nor should you feel pressured just because time passes and you feel you'll miss the ideal time to have children or be married. Love and everything that comes with it will flow and go where it should go with the right person when the time and circumstances are right.

So what do you do in the meantime? You let it flow like a river. Can you imagine trying to make a river flow in your desired direction? It would be impossible without a current to facilitate that flow. Allow a person time to build trust or whatever that person needs to feel comfortable moving forward with the relationship, especially if they are giving you what you currently need as a friend or whatever your titles are at the present moment. Love is patient and kind and doesn't require rushing or time clocks. It flows where it needs to go and grows when nurtured correctly. Everything in life requires time to prepare for readiness; plants, pregnancies, babies, teeth, hair, nails, business, friendships, careers, the list goes on and on. It does not stop when it comes to love. Everything that grows, blossoms, or prospers requires time to do so.

When we meet someone we deem worthy of our time, we start planning for the future instead of enjoying the present moment.

Once the relationship progresses, you will never get that stage back. Often we rush to the next level of the relationship, assuming if we move to the big moments, such as labeling the relationship with titles, cohabiting, having a baby, or getting married, it will solidify the relationship. The best way to solidify a relationship is to establish excellent communication and respect for each other's time and space to be just as comfortable apart as you are together. Rushing into anything usually leads to disaster.

Over my lifetime, I have spoken to and listened to many people, especially women, who were completely unsatisfied with their current relationships. However, they still desired to continue the relationship instead of nipping those issues in the bud. We can sweep things under the rug to continue moving forward with a relationship, failing to realize that one

day all those issues swept under the carpet
will have to surface; there is no way around
it. Sometimes there were things I wanted to
do, but once I was told not to do them or
didn't have a choice, it made me want to do
them even more. It reminds me of the story
of Adam and Eve; you can have everything
at your disposal and be content with it, but
once you're forbidden to partake of anything
else, the challenge gets real. There is such a
thing as two people getting together, falling in
love, and wanting to move forward with their
relationship at the same speed, without any
outside force pushing them forward. When I
was younger, I thought there wasn't enough
time to stop chasing love. However, I learned
that love flows and doesn't require force or
a chase. Two people should mutually desire
to be with each other even when things
seem like they're not moving in your desired
direction. It doesn't mean it's not moving,

but at a pace that's best for the relationship. During this time, things are adjusting and needs developing within the individuals and collectively as a couple.

Think Before You Leap

♥

When you think about all the choices that can be made in life, they usually allow you to change your mind about everything except when being sentenced by a judge for committing a crime. In that case, you typically get what the judge sentenced you to. Sometimes that sentence is a life sentence or the death penalty, depending on the state, and that's it, no way out, no getting around it. Why is marriage similar? It is one of the few things in life that requires you to say the only way out is through death. It also reminds me of a gang; the only way out is usually through death. No wonder there are so many homicides that take place among spouses.

Sure, you have the option of divorce if it doesn't work out. That's not hard to do. It's expensive, complicated, and stressful, but people fail to discuss the aftermath of a divorce. It affects not only the children involved if there are children but also the two parties involved long after the divorce. People still feel pain years after getting divorced that they can't get over. The idea of a divorce should not be taken lightly, nor should we take becoming exclusive lightly.

Suppose there was no option to divorce or break up. Would you be able to spend the rest of your life with the partner you are considering leaping into marriage or an exclusive relationship with? Do you know how they are when times are bad, such as losing a loved one to death or

imprisonment, getting sick, losing a job
or income, relocating, struggling with an
addiction, or even having kids? All of these
situations have a life-changing effect on your
personality and mood. It is not feasible to
wait until you experience all these situations
before choosing to be exclusive or getting
married. Still, it is good to truly get to
know your partner beyond the lust stage and
through real-life issues before taking that leap
over the broom. Remember, this is the rest of
your life we are discussing; until DEATH Do
you part.

At one point, saying "I do" meant forever,
which we still say until death do us part
when saying our vows, which implies it's
forever. Still, many relationships tend to part
ways before death, resulting in divorce. Some
people refuse to divorce no matter how hard
the marriage gets; they believe you stick

around and stay committed no matter what; just be encouraged because the bad days will soon be over. That may be true in some cases, but there have been numerous cases where it didn't get better but only worse. Those cases led to murder, suicide, overdose, addiction, cheating, low self-esteem, broken spirit, emptiness, and pure sadness and unhappiness. It's hard to say when it's the best time to throw the towel in because no one knows what the future holds. Still, life is short, and spending years and years in pain and agony in something that isn't working, no matter how much you try, will keep you from living a fulfilling life. These are things to consider before taking that leap, but if there are no issues, congratulations, you've made it this far.

Now that you've been dating or in an exclusive relationship for x amount of time, everything is flowing right where it should be, where you and your partner are ready to move to the next phase of your relationship without either party feeling forced. This time is exciting and calls for a celebration, but before you celebrate, reflect on all the time you spent together. Are there any loose ends or concerns that should be addressed before taking that leap? Any red flags that you dismissed because you didn't want to start an argument or be misunderstood? Anything that is an issue but you find it hard to express or discuss with your partner because you never see eye to eye on the subject matter? Is there something you haven't disclosed to your partner for fear that they may look at you differently or judge you? Are there things that could be revealed later on that can significantly impact the relationship? Are there things your partner does that annoy you that you know one day will be an issue if it continues? Is your partner just too cute or handsome for you to see past their beauty to the depth of their soul?

Taking the leap and becoming exclusive or getting married before tying all loose ends is like taking a used car on a long road trip without having a mechanic take a look at it first or without fixing things such as oil leaks, oil changes, and ensuring the tires and everything is working good before getting on the road. No one wants to be on their way to their destination to find themselves stuck on the road. This same analogy applies to marriages; no one wants to be married for five or more years and find themselves stuck on the road to divorce. Of course, this can happen regardless, but discussing pertinent information maturely and respectfully before jumping over the broom could eliminate a lot of unnecessary drama. Before marriage is an excellent time for both of you to discuss your plans for the future. Are you sure your partner can provide what your expectations are of them, or are you in love with the IDEA of what potential they have to deliver your expectations?

Many young girls, especially those who grew up in my era, dreamed of nothing else but getting married. The thought of a proposal, ring, and big wedding excites some. Still, I looked forward to the part where I cook, clean, serve, have babies, encourage, pray, and strive to be the best partner I can be to my spouse in every way I can. Unfortunately, sometimes for reasons unbeknownst to anyone, relationships end. Notice I said come to an end and not fail; I chose those words because just because a relationship ends doesn't mean it failed. It could mean you realized you weren't compatible or were growing differently. Still, regardless of the reason, it is essential to look to the future because long-term exclusive relationships or marriages after the age of 40 look a lot different than they did 20 years ago. It is essential to know that things will change for the good and the bad regardless of who you decide to take that journey with; love will have its share of ups and downs. There will be days of bliss, misunderstandings, and frustration, which is inevitable; you will experience it because it's part of growing, learning, living, and just being.

Storms are what many people like to call these experiences that cause us pain, weakness, or anxiety. So, before you become exclusive or leap, is this someone you can weather the storm with? Not someone who causes the storm but someone you can laugh or relax with; you can show respect, love, gentleness, and care, no matter the situation.

What are your individual goals? What about your goals as a couple? Are your goals aligned with each other? When leaping to become exclusive or married, it is crucial to sit and discuss what you want and where you want to be in the future.

Always remember that the person you think is incredible right now somewhere someone else thinks of them just as how you feel about your ex, which means there could come a time when this fantastic person will have you in a position that makes you feel very low, whether it's intentional or not.

Conclusion

♥

Are you just a puppy looking for an owner? Lost and looking for someone to love you? While it is natural and normal to crave love and to desire to find your soulmate or at least someone to be exclusive with, I urge you to do the work necessary first to identify who you are, love yourself, and then I assure you that you will attract the "right" person to give you what you desire and have hoped for.

Allow the tips and my experiences in this book to help you identify how you have been operating in love and to help you change your mindset, expectations, and YOUR life!

Visit my website at www.modicareign.com to learn more tips about self-discovery and relationships.

About Author

Rarchelle Massey-Smith is an author, self-care blogger, and relationship expert who is passionate about helping women of all ages become the best possible versions of themselves. As a proud mother, daughter, and sister who is committed to empowering her community, Rarchelle is always there to provide a word of advice or a helping hand to those in need.

Rarchelle wrote *Self-Discovery* to help women practice self-care, recover after an emotional breakup, and start attracting their dream partner through a mix of self-love strategies and seasoned advice. She's talented at seeing issues from multiple perspectives and helping readers identify the core beliefs or behaviours that are holding them back from achieving a happy and meaningful life.

Rarchelle holds a B.A. in Psychology, and she's worked as a manager at a Funeral Home for over a decade. In her free time, you can find her practicing natural hair and skin care, sharing a coffee with friends, and spending time with her wonderful family. For more information, visit her website at https://modicareign.com